Gaudí in the Cathedral of Mallorca

Gaudí in the Cathedral of Mallorca

Text Pere-Joan Llabrés
Photography Jordi Puig | Pere Vivas

TRIANGLE ▼ POSTALS

The cathedral of Mallorca, 'La Seu', rises like an acropolis over the sea, at the end of the bay of Palma. It dominates, the most significant and grandiose monument of the façade of the ancient city, over the waves of the Mediterranean, which, until not that long ago, lapped the wall that serves as its pedestal. Erect like a mystical wall of rock, it looks like a block of sculpted stone, a statue placed on that peak "so that the sun comes to caress it during the daytime, to fill it with white heat and light it up like a flame each sunset", wrote Santiago Rusiñol.

'La Seu' of Mallorca is a jewel of Gothic art, of perfect and majestic lines, balanced and serene, slender and one would say spiritually raised, very befitting Catalan, Mediterranean and French Midi Gothic, in accordance with this style so saturated with Christianity with which, in the early 14th century, it was started at the behest of the Good King Jaume II of Mallorca.

The interior construction took three hundred years, starting with the royal chapel and presbytery, and which was later extended until the creation of three extremely high naves: the last keystone in the vaulting of the central nave was blessed and positioned in 1587, and the main doorway was blessed in 1601. Work began on the main façade in the second half of the 19th century and completed in the early 20th century.

With the passing of time, different artistic styles have been expressed in 'La Seu' of Mallorca and adaptations of the space have been undertaken in accordance with the cultural and spiritual mentality of successive Mallorcan generations, which has always found a space for celebrating faith, of a popular religiousness and artistic creativity. The original plan of the cathedral has therefore experienced alterations that responded to a "taking root", to an involvement of the local culture in the way of taking part in the liturgy and in the different forms of spirituality and religious experience.

We will clearly notice two significant elements of art and religious celebration —which interfered with the development of the early architectural plan of space distribution— in order to orientate the Gaudian visit to the Mallorcan cathedral. The first, the large windows that should have illuminated the interior of the church and which remained bricked up until well into the 20th century; and the second, the choir stalls of the cathedral clergy which from the 16th century was positioned —like a building within another building— in the centre of the high altar, thus obstructing the view from the presbytery and the altar which appeared sunken into the apse of the royal chapel.

This is how
"La Seu" of
Mallorca shines
out, restored by
Gaudí between
1904 and 1914

Bishop Pere-Joan Campins' plan

Antoni Gaudí arrived in Mallorca on the 26th of March 1902 to carry out the restoration and decoration work that he had been entrusted with by Bishop Pere-Joan Campins i Barceló: his mission consisted of ensuring that the bright light of the Mediterranean sun entered the cathedral through the stained glass windows; restoring the royal chapel to make it suitable for holding the Holy Eucharist around the altar that also had to be moved from the back towards the central nave; restoring the old chair so that the bishop could preside over the liturgy; moving the choir from the centre of the cathedral so that the priests, the bishop's assistants, would occupy both sides of the episcopal see and finally, to prepare the two pulpits from which the gospel, read and preached, would reach the people congregated in the wide naves.

Pere-Joan Campins (1859-1915)

These were, basically, the liturgical and architectural restoration works on 'La Seu' that Bishop Campins entrusted to the brilliant architect, the "total artist", Antoni Gaudí. The Mallorcan prelate and the devout architect shared the ideals of the liturgical movement with great fervour, and which from the mid-19th century spread through France, Belgium and Germany. This movement would culminate in the Vatican II: the Constitution of the Sacred Liturgy (1963), which defended the participation of all God's people in the celebration, above all of the Eucharist, presided over by the bishop, surrounded by the priests and other ministers, around a single altar. This is, according to the abovementioned Constitution (41), the "pre-eminent manifestation of the Church", whose mystery is the symbol and pre-eminent figure in the cathedral church.

Now we will see, step by step, the artistic and restoration work in 'La Seu' of Mallorca by Antoni Gaudí.

View of the central
nave from the
chapel of the
Trinity
(19th century)

Gaudí in La Seu. 1902

The characteristic quality of 'La Seu' —stated Gaudí— "is the proportionality and harmonious correlation of dimensions", both of the interior and the exterior. In Spain and other nations there are cathedrals that surpass this one in Palma in many aspects: some in terms of size, others in ornamentation and richness of artworks and details. Very few, however, perhaps none, surpass it in beautiful and graceful proportions, in airy lightness of lines and volumes. The harmonious proportionality constitutes the "merit and main distinguishing feature of this poem written in stone".

We can now see two architectural and decorative elements as soon as we enter 'La Seu' and examine the interior: the elegance of its Gothic architecture and the decoration that Gaudí introduced to it after removing unnecessary items and filling it with light and colour.

Gaudí found this proportionality and harmony "broken and totally lost" in 'La Seu' of that time, occupied by the choir in the centre, as can be seen by the engravings before the architect's interventions. Entering by the main doorway, worshipers could not see either the altar or the bishop's chair or *cátedra*

The cathedral in a 19th century engraving

The choir in the centre of the cathedral (19th century photo)

—which provides the name Cathedral— or the main apse, or the chapel of the Trinity. An arch in Plateresque style (16th century), that Gaudí would place on the same side as the left-hand nave and alongside the Almoina doorway, in the entrance of the Vermells sacristy, formed the entrance to the choir opposite the main entrance.

On the other side, the choir was connected to the presbytery by the via sacra, where the sarcophagus of Jaume II was placed, and was flanked by the two pulpits. The chapel of the Trinity was almost totally hidden by two altarpieces, placed one in front of the other: the Baroque piece from the 18th century, dedicated to the Assumption of Saint Mary, and right behind, the Gothic piece from the 14th century, now placed over the Mirador doorway.

At the beginning of the 20th century the cathedral did not get much light because most of the large windows and rose windows were bricked up. As regards these, some of them were illuminated: the one called "High Gothic eye of medieval Christianity", open in 1370 and with stained glass from 1599, at the head of the central nave; the two that closed the side naves (open in 1898); the one that had been above the main doorway (1599), and one small one over the Almoina doorway, illuminated in 1893. The only stained glass windows were the three in the chapel of the Trinity (1898), which enabled the light to shine over the Baroque altarpiece, and the two situated on the sides of the chapel or high apse, also installed at the end of the 19th century. 'La Seu', therefore, was still dark, despite the fact that several architects had outlined many large windows in the high part of the three naves, in the royal chapel and in the sides.

This is the cathedral that Gaudí faced in 1902. Bishop Campins had called him in order to open up that marvellous building to the most honourable celebration of worship, fitted to the liturgical rules of the Roman rite, heirs of the ancient ecclesiastical tradition, with a greater participation of all the faithful, above all in the Holy Eucharist. According to the bishop, the functionalism of the celebratory space had to be accompanied by the appropriate decoration, above all by ensuring that light entered through the large windows, in particular those that had to surround the high altar within the presbytery. Just the right amount of light, that Gaudí thought appropriate for a place of worship, neither too bright nor too dark, that invited people to worship, would be the work of the brilliant architect who arrived in Mallorca in that winter of 1902.

Photo of the
interior of "La Seu"
between the
presbytery and
the choir (19th C.)

Interventions outside the cathedral

We shall start our visit at the main doorway. Before entering, however, let us recall that on the outside of 'La Seu', Gaudí and his collaborator Josep M. Jujol also left their mark. Two stone mosaics in the form of a rug, with drawings in white and dark grey, before the main doorway and that of the Almoina, already show the traits of identity specific to Gaudian work. Facing the main doorway we come across the figure of the deer drinking from the spring: this is a highly appropriate biblical symbol (Psalm 41) for the faithful who enter 'La Seu' to quench their thirst with the water of grace and of the sacraments that spring from there to give eternal life. Facing the side doorway of Almoina, a shield with four bars shows the heraldic signs of the ancient royal house of Mallorca.

J.M. Jujol
(1879-1949)

He also designed the pavement that surrounds 'La Seu', commissioned by the bishop and approved by the Palma City Council (1912), a design that, facing the three main doorways, was maintained in the 2002 reform work.

Additionally, in order to ventilate the sacristies of the chapels and other spots, Gaudí and Jujol opened up as many as ten small windows that they protected with grilles and decorated with incisions in the four sides, to give life to the stone.

Sacristy niches
decorated by Jujol

Stone carpet
facing the main
Doorway:
invitation to drink
the water of Life

At the entrance
to the "Almoina",
suggesting the coat
of arms of our
royal household

Entering 'La Seu'

After crossing the main doorway, on our left we can see the tombstone that in 1959 —the first centenary of the birth of Pere-Joan Campins— the cathedral chapter dedicated to the "holy memory" of that great bishop who restored the cathedral, re-established the episcopal chair, raised with noble simplicity the high altar and surrounded it above with a regal crown, moved the choir, which he placed between the chair and the altar, provided the faithful with a very wide nave and rediscovered the chapel of the Holy Trinity.

The Latin inscription of this grateful praise sums up for us the work that Gaudí did at the behest of Bishop Campins.

We would first like to highlight the spacious view we have of 'La Seu' from the main doorway. We are captivated by the immense majesty and sublime grandeur of the greatest space in Gothic architecture enclosed by the minimum quantity of stone, of visible matter. The proportion between the width of the naves and the slenderness and subtlety of the columns is unique.

"This is how the most imposing and dreamed-of Holy Arch on Earth stands today".
(S. Rusiñol)

Fully introducing electric light

Fourteen slender columns that form two rows support the naves of 'La Seu'. Gaudí decorated them so that they would generously illuminate the space open to the faithful, with some wrought iron rings which, as multiple candlesticks, support 16 electrically-lit candles at a height of five metres. Gaudí, making use of the advances of the time, fully introduced electricity into 'La Seu'. He knew enough about the art of wrought ironwork and of how to give it the daring, elegant and surprising forms that stirred in his imagination. He was the son of a boilermaker and the iron, in his hands, became a free, audacious and unconventional element. He made this very clear in his intervention in 'La Seu'. He began sketching the rings of the fourteen columns —called ironically trobigueres (garters) by the Mallorcans— in November 1904, and on the 30th of the same month they began work on installing them. Twelve of them were already shining brightly on the festival of the Virgin that same year.

To our left we see the chapels of the Virgin and of Saint Sebastian, patron saint of Palma. Seeing as in 1912 a fire destroyed the altarpiece of Saint Bernard, the decision was taken not to leave burning candles on the altarpieces. So Gaudí planned a row of wrought iron candlesticks hung opposite the altarpieces and attached to the side walls. The system did not work. He then forged two lanterns, one for each chapel, and which hung from both corbels painted in old gold. On the left-hand corbels, the word Roma can be read and on the right-hand ones, two different dates. In the chapel of the Virgin the date 1854 is inscribed, which is the year of the dogmatic declaration of the Immaculate Conception in the Vatican by Blessed Pope Pius IX. In the chapel dedicated to the patron saint of Palma, the date inscribed is 285, which is the year that was then attributed to the martyrdom, also in Rome, of Saint Sebastian.

Wrought iron rings with electric candlesticks on the 14 columns

Moving on along the central nave we see the grand candelabrum that Gaudí illuminated with electric light bulbs instead of the oil lamps. The light they give off is yellowish to imitate the light reproduced by the wicks that burnt in the oil. He moved this candelabrum, typical in Mallorcan churches, and which had been situated right by the entrance of the royal chapel, to the centre of 'La Seu', and he added a wrought iron double cross to it in the upper part. Another four candelabrums light up the side naves; all of them are electric and have a double cross in their upper part, also forged by Gaudí.

The large candelabrum situated in the centre of the main nave

Electric light, rose windows and large windows fill the central nave with light

Lamp of
the chapel
of the Virgin

"Rome": the corbels recall
the city where the martyr
saint Sebastian died and
the definition of the
Blessed Virgin Mary

The corbels of the gothic altarpiece

The first element that came between the bishop's chair and the altar was the Gothic altarpiece, erected at the end of the 14th century and attributed to Pere Morey. The altarpiece housed seven statues: in the centre, Saint Mary, and to the sides three male saints (John the Baptist, James the Elder and John the Evangelist) and three female saints (Mary Magdalene, Eulalia and Barbara). In the predella, the high relief work shows the Seven Joys of the Blessed Mary, mysteries that inspired a great deal of worship in the Middle Ages. The altarpiece had latticework behind the images of the saints —today the lower part can be seen— that did not completely cover the figure of the bishop or stop him from seeing who was conducting the service from the altar.

When Gaudí removed it in 1904, the upper part covered the chapel of the Trinity in the form of a grille. Perhaps it already had this use in the 14th century, or perhaps this high part was originally the back of the altarpiece, right in front of the bishop's eyes seated in his chair. Today the two parts are positioned one on top of the other.

In Gaudí's restoration, at first the removal of this altarpiece was not contemplated. Some people proposed placing it in the chapel of the Trinity, since the front part, as we have mentioned, closed off this chapel. Nevertheless, on the 4th and 5th of July 1904 the Gothic altarpiece was removed from behind the Baroque altarpiece and from above this chapel. It was placed, as we have mentioned, over the entrance of the Mirador doorway, supported on stone corbels designed by Gaudí.

The chapel of Saint Bernard

To the right of the Mirador doorway is the chapel of Saint Bernard, one of the oldest named chapels in 'La Seu'. On the 30th of August 1912 the Baroque altarpiece in which it was erected was burnt. It was the period in which Gaudí was carrying out the decorative works of 'La Seu'. The ideal that guided him, and which was also followed by his assistants, above all Joan Rubió i Bellver, was that of adapting 'La Seu' back to its early plan. Therefore the plan for the chapels was to have the opening of three large windows at the back, something that until then had not been completed in either the medieval Gothic stage, which provided the chapels with low altarpieces that would not obstruct any possible large window openings at the back (in the chapter museum you can see the Gothic altarpiece of Saint Matthew and Saint Francis, from the 14th century, of reduced height), or the Baroque period, in which the altarpieces were raised as high as the ceiling (see the neighbouring chapel of Saint Martin, also by F. de Herrera), so that the outlined windows behind were completely covered.

As a result, then, Joan Rubió designed a new altarpiece of Saint Bernard, the height of which reached only to the base of the three large back windows. It is inspired by the high altarpiece of the cathedral of Tarragona. The style is somewhere between Gothic —from which Gaudí and his collaborators started off— and Catalan modernism, so much in fashion in those days. The Mallorcan sculptor Tomàs Vila produced it in alabaster.

Gaudí suggested that, at the base of the six arches, images be placed of the six Holy Fathers of the eastern and western churches: Saint Cyril of Alexandria, Saint Basil, Saint John Chrysostom, Saint Ambrose, Saint Augustine and Saint Gregory the Great. Thus, the "last of the Holy Fathers", as many considered Saint Bernard of Clairvaux, was surrounded by who, in the eastern and western worlds, with his

Altarpiece of Saint Bernard, designed by J. Rubió i Bellver

doctrine and apostolic zeal had "given light", after the Apostles, to the Church of Christ.

The most relevant work in this chapel within the Gaudian line of restoration and decoration, however, is the opening of the three large windows at the back. The drawings are the work of the Catalan painter Darius Vilàs and were installed in 1916, when Gaudí was no longer working in Mallorca, although his collaborator and disciple Rubió i Bellver was still involved in the project. Since they were the first stained glass windows that illuminated a side chapel, great care was taken to ensure that the light was not too strong, from the centre of 'La Seu', for those who entered it. The glass panes were darkened with grisaille. This lack of light in some very valuable stained glass windows, produced in the studios of Xavier Bonet in Barcelona, has become more noticeable with the passing of time. The restored chapel was officially opened in 1921.

Two fragments of the stained glass windows can currently be seen in the chapel, started by Gaudí in 1903 and which were meant for the royal chapel. One formed the lower part of the *Regina martyrum*, with the figure of Saint Valerian, the legendary husband of Saint Cecilia and a lion's head: the other belongs to *Regina Apostolorum* and represents Saint Paul.

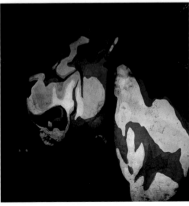

Fragments of the unfinished stained glass windows of *Regina martyrum* and *Regina apostolorum*

The two pulpits situated to the sides of the presbytery

Now we are facing the presbytery, which Gaudí moved forward as far as the first pair of columns that separate and support the naves, gaining this space in the entrance to the royal chapel.

On either side are the two pulpits, named the pulpit "of the Epistle" (on our right) and that "of the Gospel" (on the left), which the Aragonese Renaissance sculptor Juan de Salas produced between 1529 and 1531. As we have mentioned, they were situated on the two upper angles of the choir, facing the presbytery, but in a different position to the one they hold now. On our right, the large one (as was traditional in Mallorcan churches), from which the preacher gave the sermon, and on the left the smaller one.

Gaudí not only placed them at the entrance of the presbytery, facing the worshipers who listened to the call of the Epistle and the Gospel and the sermons from the naves, but also adapted their positioning in line with the liturgical rules that were then in force. He placed the large one at the side of the Gospel, and the small one to the right, where the Epistle was sung in the solemn mass services.

Gaudí, moreover, who was always very concerned about bringing the celebration of the Gospel or preaching closer to the people, provided both pulpits with a sounding board. The bigger pulpit had already shown it off in the festival of the Virgin in 1904, at which the sermon of the Pontifical Mass was given by Reverend Miquel Costa i Llobera. This sounding board, of ephemeral material (wood and fabric), but which was not lacking inventiveness, had a simple and elegant design —but which the Mallorcans called the *esclata-sang*, the saffron milk cap, a wild mushroom— and lasted until 1972, when the loudspeaker equipment rendered them redundant.

The high pulpit, its location changed by Gaudí, in which he installed a sounding board

That sounding board was provisional. Gaudí had imagined and planned one that would be an elevation and crowning of the main pulpit, full of biblical symbolism. He aimed to extend the base and body of the pulpit, supported by animals and Atlases, while around it, in low-relief, were representations of the Seven Joys of the Blessed Virgin, the four evangelists and the Holy Saints of the Western Church. Gaudí had planned to add a sculptural body that, starting from the centre of the pulpit, would be expanded with an also octagonal stone sounding board, formed by eight angels, one on each edge, with the wings open and extended towards its neighbours, formed parabolic curves. Above the angels a column would be erected with images of the twelve apostles, over which would be sculpted the symbols of the four evangelists –the tetramorphos. The series would be crowned by the globe and cross of the Saviour.

The sounding board and crowning of the small pulpit is eminently symbolic. The sculptural work by Salas only shows the Compassion of Mary, between the angel Gabriel and Our Lady of the Annunciation. Gaudí designed the stone sounding board and the large, symbolic crowning of the pulpit, whereas Tomàs Vila was entrusted with its production. In five niches in the form of half moons that open over the sounding board are the figures of the apostles: Peter (an imitation of which is found over the doorway of the old diocesan Seminary) and Paul, and another three characters (prophets or apostles). Above and as a crowning piece is a representation of the sacrifice of Abraham, "our father in faith". Isaac appears tied and leaning against his father, at the point of being sacrificed and before him can be seen the lamb that replaced him in the sacrifice (Genesis 22). The image of Christ the Saviour, of who Isaac was a figure, and the cross where Christ offered his only and definitive sacrifice crown the pulpit of the Epistle. It is in fact the Epistle that was the first reading of mass, sung in the solemn mass, and was a fragment of the apostolic writings (above all of Paul and Peter) or of the Old Testament (prophets or history of Israel, in which Abraham's sacrifice is a key event and prophecy).

Sounding board of the pulpit of the Epistle: the sacrifice of Abraham; apostles and prophets

(previous page) The high pulpit with the sounding board (the "saffron milkcap mushroom"). Photo prior to 1912

The galleries for the singers

Gaudí thought of the liturgy as a rule and source of the highest form of aesthetics. He thought that hymns and music played a very important role within it. As we have seen, he was very concerned with achieving good acoustics. The hymn of the *schola cantorum* and also that of the people were very highly regarded by this "total artist". Moreover, the year of the restoration of 'La Seu' was the same year that saw the start of the renovation of the liturgical hymn from the Gregorian and of promoting polyphony increasingly more in accordance with the strict dignity of the celebrations. The popular hymn, adapted to the liturgical rules and in the local language, was also included in the renovated pastoral work of Bishop Campins, above all due to the Motu proprio of Saint Pius X, of the 22nd of November 1903. The prelate and the God-serving architect were in full agreement in all matters regarding the promotion and appreciation of the hymn of all the people in liturgical celebrations. On the other hand, in the abovementioned document, the Pope recommended that, if the singers had to be situated before the people, they would undertake their task from behind the latticework.

On either side of the altar and the presbytery, between the choir where the cathedral clergy sang, with special responsibility for the liturgical hymn, and the great congregation of the faithful, Gaudí placed the two singers' galleries for the choir, built with remains of the "building" and from the Renaissance ornamentation from the choir that had been in the centre of 'La Seu', from the "corridor of candles" —withdrawn from the royal chapel and which he used for the two ceilings—, from gilded statuettes of angels and other Baroque elements that accompanied the 18th-century altarpiece, and other new pieces that he designed himself (latticework

The right-hand side of the singers' gallery: consoles with the musical notes *re* and *mi*

and consoles with the liturgical hymn of Saint John the Baptist which was the origin of musical notes (*Ut queant laxis...*), highlighting the following notes with gilded letters: *ut, re, mi, fa, sol, la*). Only the one situated alongside the main pulpit —which provided excellent acoustics— was still used for the schola cantorum of the Seminary until 1968, which Bishop Campins had built mainly for the liturgical service of the 'La Seu'.

Gaudí also had the stone stairs that lead to the singers' gallery built, and the grilles and handrails that closed and gave access to the singers' gallery. Three doors and three handrails for the benches on the lower part of the gallery adjacent to the chapel of Saint Peter and three handrails on the gallery beside the *Corpus Christi* provide another amazing spectacle of the art of wrought ironwork done with mastery and creativity. The stairway that rises from the chapel of Saint Peter to the singer's gallery, built with material reused from the Renaissance choir, is a marvellous example of the unique character of Gaudian work.

The restoration architect began building these galleries —which ironically the critics called "tramways"— on the 12th of November 1904.

Months before, on the 16th of July, Gaudí had had placed, on both sides of the presbytery, now lengthened as far as the central nave, the stone benches called "the concelebrants" benches, which had previously flanked the Baroque altarpiece. They were situated in the lower part of the galleries, facing each other.

Door and railing in wrought iron in the left-hand singers' gallery

Baroque elements, ceiling of the "corridor of candles", the musical note fa, in the left-hand singers' gallery

The railing at the entrance of the presbytery

It is truly one of the most beautiful and suggestive works of Gaudian wrought iron art. It has absolutely nothing in common with the majority of grilles that close and ostentatiously separate the presbyteries of some Spanish cathedrals. It is not a grille, but rather two candelabras with a total of six high candlesticks and sixteen low ones, which seem to some extent inspired by the two large Baroque candelabras by Joan Matons (1718) on exhibition in the chapter museum. The handrail protects the entrance to the presbytery with a system that enables it to be opened and closed easily. In the centre of the handrail Gaudí cast the anagram of Saint Mary (a very graceful M), the incumbent saint of 'La Seu'. Four medallions hang from the lower part of the two candelabras: two with the four bars of the kings of Mallorca and two with the castle over the sea and the palm: the two heraldic symbols that make up the coat of arms of the city and Kingdom of Mallorca. Today, the six high candles are lit for the celebration of the Holy Eucharist; in the more solemn services all twenty-two candles are lit.

With this handrail, the presbytery is not closed but rather artistically decorated: it does not break the continuity between the clergymen taking part in the celebration from the choir (often today also occupied by secular and religious believers) and the congregation seated in the wide naves. In fact, at large services a crown of believers in Christ is formed around the altar of the Eucharist: from the bishop who presides from the chair to the believers who watch and follow the liturgical service from the wide naves as far as the main doorway. In this way the unity of the assembly is made visible, a manifestation of the Church, "sacrament of unity", congregated by its pastor and associated with the only table of the Word and the bread of Life.

Wrought iron railing of the presbytery; castle over the sea, the coat of arms of Palma

On the right-hand side of the presbytery, alongside the candelabra, and present since the Chrism Mass 2001, is the ambo from which the Holy Scripture is read and proclaimed. It was designed by the architect of the Sagrada Família, Jordi Bonet, and inspired by the lecterns that Gaudí made for the 'La Seu'. It combines the wrought iron of the structure with the wood that supports the Lectionary, the base also being of oak. An innovative detail that distinguishes it is the recipient for flowers situated at the height of the book, facing the congregation. It is a reminder that the biblical reading, before the assembly, spreads the fine odour of Christ and scatters the spirit of brotherhood and joy among the faithful. During the Easter period the Easter candlestick is placed alongside the ambo, a facsimile of the one Gaudí designed for the Sagrada Familia, made in 2001: the column is made of red porphyry.

(previous page) An ingenious device (with the letter "M" of Mary) opens the centre of the railing

The area for celebrating the Holy Eucharist decorated with candelabras. Medallion with the coat of arms of our kings

The high altar

From the theological and liturgical, historical and artistic point of view, the high altar is the most notable monument in 'La Seu' of Mallorca. It is supported by nine columns, the central one of which is Byzantine, chiselled out to house reliquaries and, therefore, designed specifically for an altar. The other eight are late Romanesque or Cistercian, or perhaps Mudejar. It is quite likely that it was the high altar of the cathedral-mosque, consecrated by the second bishop of Mallorca, Pere de Morella, in 1269. The *cap nou* (main apse) of 'La Seu' was dedicated to him by Bishop Berenguer Batle on the 1st of October 1346, on its official opening for worship, work having commenced at the beginning of the 14th century. It was once again consecrated by Bishop José de Cepeda in 1746, when it was moved due to the installation of the large Baroque altarpiece, and finally on Sunday the 1st of October 1905 by Bishop Campins, after Gaudí had positioned it where it can be seen today. The architect, greatly imbued with the spirit of the liturgical movement and indoctrinated by his "master of liturgy", Bishop Campins, understood from the beginning of his restoration work that the high altar could not remain "hidden" at the back of the royal chapel or attached to an altarpiece, as Gothic and Baroque art had done to it. Therefore he removed the two altarpieces that would overshadow the excellence of the altar and placed it at the entrance of the royal chapel, after advancing the presbytery, as we have already mentioned. In this way the altar, visible from almost any part of 'La Seu', in the middle of the choir and before all God's people, truly became "the centre where the attention of the assembled faithful spontaneously converges", as the General Instruction of the Roman Missal stipulates (number 299), on regulating the celebration of the Holy Eucharist reviewed by the II Vatican Council.

The high altar where the eyes of all the worshippers converge

Thus in 1904 Gaudí left us with the altar almost ready for holding the post-conciliar mass. Advancing it just 1.55 m on the 22nd of February 2001, our high altar was ready for worship before the people. Gaudí placed it over the three liturgical altar steps, according to the regulations in force at the time.

Four musician angels surround the altar

In November 1904, the Olesa family, at the behest of the Chapter, returned six statuettes of angels to 'La Seu' that in 1731 had been removed from the presbytery when the Baroque altarpiece of the Assumption had been built. Gaudí wanted to place them again: four (musician angels) in the four corners of the liturgical altar steps and two (thurifers) close to the episcopal chair. They are high quality 14th-century Gothic statues.

Gaudí placed them over its jasper columns, on a base of local stone, designed by Gaudí himself, and surrounded the angels with some wrought iron candelabras that support eight candlesticks. With these, Gaudí once again showed his great skill as a wrought iron worker. His art has left us with some candelabras that illuminate —now with electric light— the Eucharistic table and which seem to support or make descend towards the altar the singular hanging baldachin. From the Acts of the Apostles (20, 8), the burning and joyous light shone over the chamber where the "breaking of the bread" was held. With so many points of light surrounding the altar, Gaudí ensured, with his wonderful creativity, that this apostolic tradition was revived in the early 20th century.

Musician angels
surround the altar
and serve as
candlesticks

The baldachin

At the Pontifical Mass of the Virgin in 1904, the altar was still covered with a simple and elementary baldachin, which responded exactly to the early idea of this decorative element of oriental origin and included in civil and religious monuments in the western world since ancient times. "Baldachin" comes from the word Baldac, the ancient name of the city that today we call Baghdad, which was famous for manufacturing tapestries. The baldachin was originally a simple tapestry that covered a throne, a distinguished sepulchre or, in Christian churches, the altar. It would emphasise the importance of the monument or the person it covered. It evolved in form when the canopy came to be supported by four columns: it often also adopted the form of an inverted Greek or Roman cup: the name ciborium by which it was also known comes from here. As we have mentioned, Gaudí returned to the origins by hanging a tapestry, like a canopy, over the altar, that was suspended from the vaulting by a metallic rod and attached to the walls of both sides by means of two cables to avoid it from moving.

The current baldachin was installed for the festival of the Virgin in 1912. Gaudí designed it simply as a model of ephemeral material, except for the back end of the heptagonal crown, which is made of iron and glass. The rest is made of wood, cardboard, paper and papier-mâché, some fabrics, chains and cords. It has been said that the architect was inspired by the baldachin in the cathedral of Hildesheim. The high part of the crown is adorned with wheatears, and with bunches of grapes and vine shoots on the lower part, in allusion to the Eucharistic bread and wine. The crown is raised slightly forward, facing the central nave and in the upper part stands a multicoloured cross with the crucified —an old very good quality statue— flanked by Mary and John the Evangelist, papier-mâché images. Thus the cross with Christ raised over the altar overlooks the grand assembly.

The fantastic baldachin, hanging from the vaulting, which projects out towards the main nave

Thirty five lamps hang from the crown. Gaudí made the baldachin, also leaning slightly towards the naves, from old fabrics and embroideries. To attach it, for each of the four sides he made a wrought iron structure, with notable adornments above and below the tapestry. Until the nineteen-sixties, the centre boasted a late 17th-century embroidery that carried an image of a pelican, a traditional Eucharistic symbol. Between the chains and cords that support the baldachin from the vaulting there are ten polyhedrons that contain a wooden and paper sphere, from which a figure descends with the form of a flame, painted red and yellow. This flame and the letters SS (*Spiritus Sanctus*) drawn in the inner part of the crown clearly show that the baldachin is a symbol of the Holy Spirit. It came to be, visibly and transformed into art, the invocation (Epiclesis), which is pronounced in the Eucharistic prayer, with which God is asked to send the down Holy Spirit over the offerings and over the assembly to form the body of Christ, the Lord, in the same way as the Spirit descended and came into Mary so that the Word would become flesh in her (Luke 1:35). The crown of the baldachin is heptagonal: the seven gifts of the Holy Spirit and the seven sacraments. Seven is the number of plenitude, the plenitude of grace that the Spirit instils in the Church.

The whole baldachin (crown, lamps, polyhedrons...) was illuminated electrically by Gaudí, which strengthened the sense of festival provided by the altar lamps that traditionally surrounded the celebration of the Holy Eucharist. Hanging from the vaulting, the baldachin appears to rest over the columns crowned by the musician angels, adapted as candlesticks.

Many people have thought of this provisional baldachin as the most impressive piece of work by Gaudí in 'La Seu': it is a spatial, free and rhythmic sculpture. It was slightly restored in 1998.

baldachin, stained
glass windows
and candelabrums
provide light,
colour and a
festive atmosphere
to the main nave

Solid material:
metal and glass,
with wheatears
and vine shoots

The crucifix
that presides over
all of "La Seu"
from above the
baldachin

Thirty five lamps recall
the Acts of the Apostles
(20:8): "In the room
where we had met
(to break bread) there
were many oil lamps"

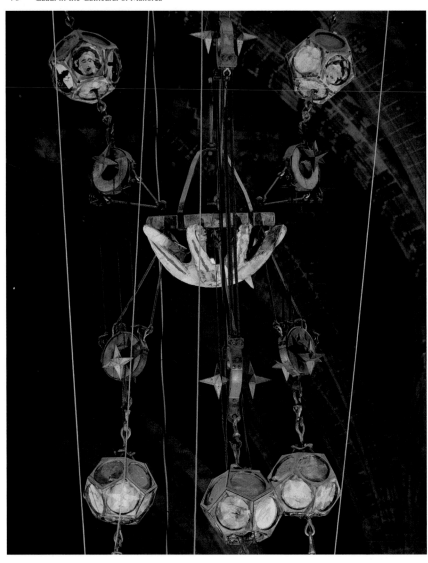

The baldachin
symbolises the
Holy Ghost: a
flame descends
over the altar

The old corridor of candles and the new illumination

Moving the choir from the centre of the main nave to the royal chapel was one of the aims of the restoration that Bishop Campins had commissioned Gaudí to carry out, but it was also to decorate and enhance the beauty of such an important and meaningful space in 'La Seu' from an artistic and liturgical point of view.

The royal chapel had had the corridor of candles since 1327. It was a kind of wooden row of balconies, carved in their lower part like Mudejar coffering. The candles were placed on the parapet that led to the inside of the chapel, and burnt and illuminated the setting in the big solemnities. We have a representation of it in oils, which shows the decoration of the presbytery of 'La Seu' for the festivals dedicated to the Immaculate Conception in 1856. The corridor of candles surrounded the royal chapel and was raised in line with the upper part of the episcopal chair.

The restoration report (project), passed by the Cathedral Chapter on the 14th of November 1903, did not include plans to withdraw this corridor, but rather place it at a convenient height over the choir stalls and close to the lower part of the large windows so that the stained glass windows could be controlled and looked after from this point. It began to be dismantled on the 12th of July, however. We have already mentioned that parts of its remains were reused by Gaudí for the ceiling of the two singers' galleries. Other fragments are found in the Diocesan Museum and others, unfortunately, have been scattered and lost.

Gaudí planned and completed a new illumination for the presbytery, the choir and the royal chapel. Replacing the corridor of candles, he placed 12 candelabras on the side walls painted in old gold, with six electrified candles on each one and distributed from the entrance of the main apse as far as the bishop's chair.

Fragments
of the "corridor
of candles" reused
in the two singers'
galleries

Where he most developed his skills as an innovative and creative artist was in the five lamps in the form of fantastic crowns, which shine out and illuminate from above the royal chapel, beneath the two stained glass windows that flank it and over the two small side chapels of the choir. The largest lamp takes the form of a tiara, with three attractive rings in the upper part; the two medium-sized lamps have two rings and the other two smaller ones just one. The fine metallic structure supports numerous brightly coloured light bulbs. These five lamps-cum-crowns make up, along with the baldachin and the ceramic decoration around the cathedral, the most stunning Modernist proclamation —or rather Gaudian— decoration of our "Seu".

One of the candelabras that replaced the "corridor of candles"

The "tiara": fantastic candelabrum in the upper part of the Trinity

Rose window and two stained glass windows in the royal chapel

The restoration report for 'La Seu' (November 1903) firstly mentions the opening of the walled up large windows in the royal chapel. Many people thought that it would be better to complete the work on them and install the stained glass in them before moving the choir.

In fact, it seems that as soon as Gaudí arrived in Mallorca and was settled in the episcopal palace as a guest of Bishop Campins, he enthusiastically set about preparing the stained glass windows that, according to the bishop's plan, had to fill the main apse with light. The last invocations of the Laurentian litany would outline the programme. If this had been undertaken in full, we would now have expressed the invocations of the Queen of the angels, of the patriarchs, of the prophets, of the apostles, of the martyrs, of the confessors, of the virgins, of the Holy Rosary and of the Queen conceived free of stain of original sin.

Gaudí began manufacturing and made stained glass combination tests. The first test was almost certainly the stained glass window he had built for the old oratory of Saint Paul in the episcopal palace and which he dedicated to the Mallorcan bishop. It is a "religious interpretation" of the prelate's coat of arms: over a field with pine trees (Campins), in the sea of the lower part are Jesus and Saint Peter in a boat that has the sails up. It had to be reinstalled in this oratory, in the Diocesan Museum, after the restoration work carried out in 2002 by the Fundació Caixa de Catalunya.

He was not completely satisfied with this first test. So he decided to perfect his art as constructor of stained glass windows by inventing his own system of "trichromy". The innovation consisted of using three panes of glass to obtain the desired colour. The half shades and nuances were obtained by graduating

The rose window of the Queen and the angels over the chapel of the Trinity

the three primary colours in the three layers of glass, dispensing with the enamel and leaving an empty space between the layers of glass. A fourth matt glass window toned down the colours.

Gaudí commissioned the illustrations for the stained glass windows to the painters Iu Pasqual, Jaume Llongueres and Joaquim Torres. Of course, the brilliant artist took great pains in directing the production of the drawings. In 1903 he was already taking photos of people and places in Mallorca so that its stained glass windows would really be "autochthonous", with shapes befitting the area and not from abroad, something that he reproached in the stained glass windows with central European models placed in 'La Seu'.

By November 1904, the new panes of the skylight at the back of the royal chapel were installed: *Regina Angelorum;* each space of the stone drawing was occupied by an angel's face. Bishop Campins paid for it. In January 1905, the stained glass windows of the confessors and the virgins were made, also at the Amigó company in Barcelona, and which would be placed the following August, not exactly where they are found today, but in the second large window on each side of the chapel of the Trinity. In the nineteen-eighties they were restored by Pere Cànovas (the author, between 1982 and 1989, of the six large windows that Gaudí did not manage to produce) and placed in the first large window of each side of the abovementioned chapel, precisely in the area most seen from the central nave.

Gaudí's most important piece of glazed work: stained glass windows of the *Queen of confessors* and *Queen of virgins*

The moving of the choir

We have already seen that this was one of the priorities in the restoration of 'La Seu', without doubt the most important according to Bishop Campins and his advisors, chiefly Canon Mateu Rotger. Our cathedral was not designed to have the choir in the centre, as occurred in many medieval Spanish cathedrals. Its early design, stated Campins, followed the arrangement of the ancient chambers of Christian celebrations: in the centre, the altar; in the apse, the bishop's chair, surrounded by the clergy seated on both sides; the congregation of the faithful was situated in the nave. Recent historical studies do not confirm exactly the early plan that Campins surmised in the cathedral of Mallorca and which he had seen in the grand old churches in the south of France and Italy, when he had made the "ad limina" visit. What is true, however, is that the vicissitudes in the construction of our "Seu", started with the apse and chapel of the Trinity by Jaume II around 1300 and extended to three naves some thirty years later, resulted in a very deep central apse (unlike what other Hispanic cathedrals of the era usually possessed), to which could be moved, without too much difficulty, the solidly erected choir in the centre of 'La Seu' in the 16th century.

On the 19th of June 1904, with the restoration works plan completed, the report and model presented to and passed by the bishop and the Chapter, Joan Rubió i Bellver arrived, Gaudí's first assistant on the works on 'La Seu', and the next day work was started on knocking down the walls of the retrochoir that led to the main doorway. The works continued at a good rate. By the 27th work had already started on taking down the Baroque altarpiece and later on the Gothic altarpiece was removed. On the 12th of July they proceeded on the work that left the royal chapel free, and then began to position the steps of the presbytery advanced towards the central nave. In October, the main apse was already prepared to receive the choir stalls with its 110 seats.

The 16th-century choir stalls placed on either side of the chair

On the 3rd of November, Gaudí, who had arrived on the 28th of October, now organised the installation of the choir in the royal chapel.

The choir stalls, made in the 16th century, were in late Gothic style with Renaissance elements. Gaudí put the Renaissance ornamentation by Juan de Salas (the upper frieze of the choir stalls, the small columns and the corbels of the backs) in the singers' galleries. He preserved, of course, the high relief work of a biblical nature —the work of the French artists Philippe Filla and Antoine Dubois, who sculpted, alternately, passages from the Old and New Testaments, according to the programme of Canon Gregori Genovard (1514)— which runs along the high part of the backs; he replaced the crowning of the choir stalls with neo-Gothic decoration, made by Mallorcan carpenters, and added some elements of his own creation to it.

Towards the end of his intervention, finally interrupted in 1914, Josep M. Jujol painted the front part of the choir to counter the darkness of the walnut wood, and fragmentarily gilded some high relief work, backs and cresting, as well as the right-hand door at the back. It is perhaps the most controversial decoration for some people and the most appreciated by others: we refer here to the brightly coloured painting of the front parts of the seat backs on the right-hand side. The iconographic programme of Jujol's paintings was based on the Passion of Christ, whose passages with their corresponding prophesies are sculpted in the upper frieze. The back of the first seat to the right of the chair is decorated with the initials JHS (Jesus the Saviour of Men) with the cross over the H. The Latin words refer to the text of the Gospel of Luke (22: 44): the drops of sweat as the blood of Jesus, in the prayer on the Mount of Olives, fall onto the earth,

which flowers like a meadow in spring. It means the regeneration of the world from the blood of Jesus Christ. Further on the flag of the resurrection unfolds: the triumph of the Lord over death, which is the beginning of the new creation. The illumination of the choir with optic fibre was installed between 1997 and 1998.

Incisions by Jujol in a choir lectern

The back of the choir, ceramics and paintings by Jujol

To liven up the
darkness of the
walnut wood, Jujol
painted the vivid
blood of Christ
the Redeemer

In the corner,
the standard
of the Resurrection

The high relief work
over the Passion of
Christ, decorated
with gold by Jujol,
inspired his paintings
below.

The episcopal chair

Bishop Berenguer Batle, who consecrated the high altar in 1346, made a donation of the stone chair that he placed beneath the chapel of the Trinity, at the back of the royal chapel. His coat of arms (two parrots) was carved into the niche that houses the chair. For centuries the bishops of Mallorca "made their place" in this chair during the Pontifical Masses, as recorded in the chapter rules and other old books. The 15th-century Gothic altarpiece partially hid the chair and the 18th-century Baroque altarpiece ended up covering it completely. The bishop presided from his chair in the choir, and from there, by the via sacra, advanced towards the altar in the Eucharistic liturgy. One of Bishop Campins' greatest concerns on deciding to restore 'La Seu' was that of uncovering and reusing "the pontifical Chair or See". Evidence of this is that, immediately after Gaudí's first visit in March 1902, the boards of the old stone chair were freed and it was photographed.

This episcopal chair maintained its early position, which corresponded to it in accordance with the distribution of space in the old cathedrals, but it was enhanced and decorated with seven steps and an attractive ornamentation that provided it with an extraordinary elegance.

On the 22nd of September 1904 work began on the construction of the stairway, from local stone, that went up to the chair: it was completed on the 29th of October. On either side of the chair, attached to the third step, were placed the two jasper columns with the Gothic thurifer angels, also surrounded by wrought iron candlesticks, like those of the high altar. These two columns were also decorated with coloured drawings. Part of the Gothic adornment of the chair were gilded by Jujol, who left notes of drawings in charcoal for the wall of the niche, a sign of unfinished work.

The stone chair 14th century) restored and used again by Bishop Campins 7/8-12-1904)

On the upper part and on both sides of the chair, Gaudí and Jujol shaped some gilded letters, hardly legible, that came from the old Roman pontifical (in the part relating to the ordination of bishops) and which, translated from the Latin, say, "Give him, Lord, the episcopal chair, so that he may govern our Church and the people that you have entrusted to him".

In the high part of the stairway, as a balustrade, Gaudí installed two symmetrical handrails in gilded wrought iron, which leave the way free in front and along the two sides.

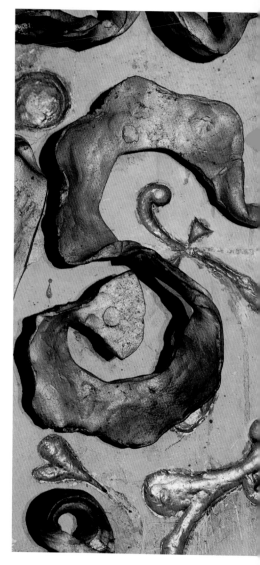

The chair
decorated by Jujol

Detail of the
inscription
designed by Jujol

Charcoal drawing
of planned but
unrealised work
by Jujol

The chair overlooking the choir. Below, two benches for the cantors

Two thurifer angels with candlesticks on either side of the chair

(next page) Wrought iron railings close to the chair

The ceramic decoration

The ceramic work of Antoni Gaudí really stands out, being rich in forms, colours and symbols. The most efficient collaborator in giving life and colour to his work was Josep M. Jujol. Between 1908 and 1909, Jujol and Gaudí completed the ceramic wall covering which surrounded the chair above the choir stalls and the two angular shells. The decoration is basically plant motifs and heraldic, with stars, the cross of Saint Eulalia (or Saint Andrew) repeated and figures that often appear in Gaudian decoration. Some palms —or olive shoots, according to interpretations— frame the coats of arms of the Bishops of Mallorca from Ramon de Torrelles through to Campins (and Doménech), drawn, however, with freedom of imagination.

The olive tree has been related to the wheatears and grapes of the baldachin. In this way the three elements of the sacraments of the Church would have been brought together: bread, wine and oil. There are a host of golden reflections with red and green glazes over white. It is a startling ornamentation, bold and attractive, over a Gothic walnut choir stall, a decorative form that the two artists must surely have planned to extend along the walls of the royal chapel, as the unfinished polychrome and gilded drawings show, along with the letters that escape from the central wall and from its sides towards the side walls, and which even cover the back part of the niches of the three saints on the left.

The fantastic decoration by Jujol at the back of the choir and around the chair

Stars, olive or palm
shoots, the cross of
Saint Eulalia: a
festival of gold and
sparkling colours

(next page)
Coat of arms
of Ramon de
Torrelles (d. 1266)
with the "J",
signature of Jujol

Coats of arms
of the bishops
of Mallorca from
Torrelles to
Domènec,
Campins' successor

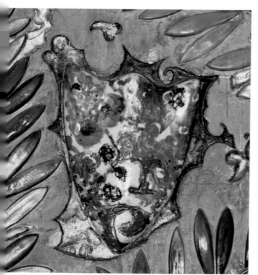

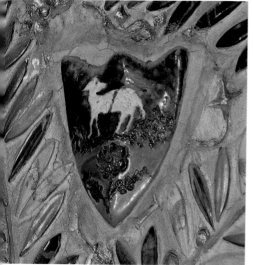

The Gothic images of the medieval altarpiece

With the 14th-century altarpiece removed and placed over the entrance of the Mirador doorway, Gaudí found an excellent destination for its seven images. That of its incumbent, Saint Mary, was positioned on the 26th of November 1904 in the chapel of the Trinity, from where the altarpiece of the three divine persons (the Holy Ghost also in human form), placed there since the 16th century. The Virgin of 'La Seu', with the left-hand side open so that it could serve as sacrarium, was, in the 14th century, the "devout invention" of the cathedral in order to guard the Holy Sacrament. According to a medieval antiphony, it meant that That to who "all the universe cannot contain and was enclosed in your womb (of the Virgin Mary) created as man". Many parish and conventual churches in Mallorca followed the example of 'La Seu' and still conserve a dozen of these images of Virgin-Sacrarium.

The saints —the two Johns and Saint James the Elder— were placed over the old small chapel of saint Gabriel, to the left of the choir, over three pedestals, designed by Gaudí —and that of the evangelist saint polychromed by Jujol—, and beneath small neo-Gothic gilded canopies, the work of Mallorcan craftsmen led by the restorer architect, who, above all in the cathedral choir, showed up to what point he appreciated and to some extent imitated the grace of Gothic art. At the same time, the three female saints symmetrically occupy the opposite part, over the chapel of Saint Eulalia, which today leads to the sacristy.

The saints Magdalene, Eulalia and Barbara, from the Gothic altarpiece, placed by Gaudí over the right-hand part of the choir

Our Virgin of 'La Seu', with the sacrarium open on the left-hand side (14th century). Gaudí ensured that it would dominate La Seu from the chapel of the Trinity

The chapel of the Trinity and its royal sepulchres

One of the projects that Bishop Campins most yearned for was the restoration of the chapel of the Trinity. Revealing and demonstrating the Gothic, slender lines of this original construction of 'La Seu', and the august mystery (Trinity and Eucharist) that the prelate surmised in it, was one of the most important objectives of the restoration of 'La Seu' of Mallorca. He also wanted to place there the remains of the kings Jaume II —which had been in a neo-classical sarcophagus between the presbytery and the choir— and Jaume III, which he himself had brought from the cathedral of Valencia in 1905. He thus fulfilled the desire of the son of Jaume I, who had chosen this chapel as mausoleum of the kings of Mallorca.

Gaudí undertook the restoration and decoration project of the Trinity. Along with Jujol he started by attaching nine pieces of blue, golden and greenish ceramic spheres (with some drawings or notes around) to the vaulting, which bear witness to restoration begun but not completed due to the interruption of both artists' work on 'La Seu' in 1914. The restoration of the Trinity was not in fact competed until 1947, and the artist behind its finalisation was the Mallorcan architect Gabriel Alomar.

As mentioned above, as well as placing the statue of the Virgin-Sacrarium in this chapel, Gaudí placed just in the threshold, hanging between the two columns that flanked its entrance over the royal chapel, a gilded wrought iron support that holds seven old golden brass candlesticks. It is an excellent and ingenious piece of work by that great artist of iron. It forms a balustrade in the chapel of the Trinity and they represent the seven golden candlesticks that shone before the Lord glorified in the sanctuary of heaven, according to the Apocalypse (1:12-20).

The Virgin-Sacrarium, the incumbent of "La Seu", overlooks the chapel of the Trinity

Drawings from the project are preserved, work of the architect Guillermo Reynés, and photographs of the models of the two royal sepulchres. The sepulchres had to be placed where the current ones are now, sculpted by Frederic Marès between 1946 and 1947. The Gaudian project of the sepulchre of Jaume II carried the silhouette of the castle of Bellver above, with an angel flying over it; the letters of Jaume II could be discerned within the walls and over the map of a city; three mullioned windows surrounded and displayed the stone coffin. The sepulchre of Jaume III had only two openings. The figures of the king and a bishop crowned it, who receives a flowering rod from the monarch, a symbol of the "Palatine Laws", which the ill-fated last king of the royal house of Mallorca had written up.

Gaudí also projected an iconographic representation of the Trinity, which, as an altarpiece, must have adorned the chapel.

Seven lamps at the entrance of the chapel of the Trinity recall the chandeliers of the Apocalypse (chapter 1)

In the vaulting of the Trinity, ceramic decoration in 'trencadís' mosaic, begun by Jujol

The doorway of Saint Jeronimo

The report, presented to the bishop and the Chapter in November 1903, scheduled several works to open entrances and connections between the chambers of 'La Seu'. The most notable and clearest for the people was the opening of an entrance through the chapel of Saint Jeronimo, alongside the cloister. Work was carried out on it with great perseverance in November 1904. The public access had previously been closed, and was in San Bernat Street, since the door forced people to enter via the choir. Gaudí had to empty out part of the left-hand wall of the chapel to let pass those people who entered or left by the same side as the base of the altarpiece. He adorned the concave section with a tombstone made from local stone, on which three crosses were sculpted.

Concavity and three crosses in stone in the doorway of Saint Jeronimo (1904)

The liturgical furnishings

 Given that both Campins and Gaudí were always aware of the "sanctity and splendour" of liturgical worship, 'La Seu' preserves an extremely valuable series of furnishings for use in religious celebrations.

The confessionary
The pews for the worshipers
The faldstool
The concelebrants' bench
The cantors' bench
Easter candle candelabra
The four stools
The stairway for the display of the Holy Sacrament in the high altar
The lecterns
The ciborium
The tintinabulum

The confessionary
Wood
426 x 150 x 213 cm

Entering by the Mirador doorway, on the left we see the main confessionary of 'La Seu'. This confessionary was also designed by Gaudí and is similar to those he himself built for the Sagrada Família in Barcelona.

The confessionary
of the penitentiary
canon
Detail: the symbol
of power of the
keys to open and
close the doors of
the Church

The pews for the worshipers
Wood
125 x 384 x 57 cm

We can also see in the naves of 'La Seu', now disperse, the pews that Gaudí designed for the worshipers. They can be easily distinguished from the others (some Gothic or very old, others more recent, from the late 20th century, because at each end of the pew and on the back they have the two panels that project out and end in a lobular figure.

In these and other wooden works that we see, Gaudí showed both his genius and his creative ability. Wood was a material that the brilliant architect appreciated greatly for its ductility and resistance.

The faldstool
Oak wood, gilded bronze and leather
82 x 86 x 48 cm

We make mention of it, above all, because it is a true jewel of furniture art by Gaudí. Prescribed for the Roman Mass of bishops for when the pontiff sat before the altar to bestow the holy orders, that which Gaudí left us is of polychromed wood and sinuous forms, with a smooth gilded and polychromed leather seat, foldable and backless, as the rules prescribed.

The seat has eight ends: the four below and in the form of a lion's paw and those above are four spheres over small Solomonic columns. Gaudí made another similar one for the Sagrada Família.

The concelebrants' bench
Oak wood and wrought iron
96 x 209 x 65 cm

The concelebrants' bench was for the priest celebrating the solemn mass, assisted then by the deacon and sub-deacon and, if he was a canon, by an attending presbyter. It thus had room for four people. The bench has all the identifying marks of Gaudian work: it is upright and comfortable. It is made of wood, with some plaited and tensed wrought iron strips. It is worth mentioning that this bench, according to the liturgical rules of the time, was used for resting (during the singing of the Kyries, the Gloria and the Credo, as well as during the sermon), and not for presiding over. In accordance with the spirit and letter of the postconciliar regulation, at Easter 2001 a presidential chair was inaugurated for the celebrant priest, made from a chair that Gaudí built for the Sagrada Família of Barcelona. From this chair, now in the church museum, Francesc Fajula carved two facsimiles where the first two concelebrants sit; whereas the chair of the main celebrant maintains Gaudí's style, is bigger and bears the coat of arms of the cathedral

Chapter on the back: Saint Mary with the infant, seated on a throne and surrounded by the words "Mary, seat of wisdom". The same sculptor has also built another seat for the bishop, for when he presides from one side of the altar facing the congregation, bigger still and with the image of the Good Shepherd on the back: it carries the inscription "Shepherd, priest, master", the three headings of the episcopal ministry.

The cantors' bench
Wood
59 x 251 x 54 cm

As well as the concelebrants' bench, Gaudí made two benches for the cantors. He followed the guidelines of the concelebrants' bench, in a simpler style. He placed them in
the centre of the choir, just below the chair, in the spot where the benefices and cantors intoned and kept up the choral liturgical chant.

Easter candle candelabra

Marble, wrought iron, copper and wood
184 x 52 x 52 cm

The Easter candle candelabra must be
added to the these authentic Gaudí furnishings, a facsimile of the one the architect
made for the Sagrada Família of Barcelona,
which is now used for the crypt parish. It
was first used in the 2001 Easter vigil. It is
a wonder of art and ingenuity: the adornments and wrought iron mechanisms ena-
ble four ministers to carry it in procession;
a brass plate on the upper part can carry
flowers. The column is made of porphyry,
a unique item in Mallorca of this highly
valued stone that comes from Persia. The
porphyry is a gift from the work of the
Sagrada Família, where the large columns
surrounding the presbytery are lines with
this stone. This reproduction was commissioned to and directed by the current
architect of the Barcelona temple, Mr.
Jordi Bonet i Armengol.

The four stools
Oak wood
47 x 50 x 50 cm

Four stools, for the presbyter and the deacons in honour of the Pontifical Mass, completed the chairs produced by Gaudí for the liturgical celebration. They coincide stylistically with the benches previously described. The inverted Y-shaped upper frame follows the same serration and the same position as the buttresses outside 'La Seu'.

The stairway for the display of the Holy Sacrament in the high altar
Polychromed wood, wrought iron and felt
180 x 135 x 235 cm

It is without doubt the most sumptuous piece of furniture designed by Gaudí for 'La Seu', a stunning piece of art in wood, wrought iron and fantastic polychrome that the brilliant artist left in 'La Seu'. The stairway can be folded away when not being used for worship (it is currently only used on the day of the Corpus Christi)). It was adapted to the back part of the altar, just as it had been placed over the three "liturgical" steps in the remodelled presbytery. The lower part rests on the floor and the high part is firmly supported over the last step by means of two arms. On the upper part there is a small step from where the minister placed the chalice with the consecrated form in the high monstrance for greater Eucharistic show. The stairway is in polychromed wood, with wrought iron handrails in fantastic forms, decorated with the four-barred coat of arms and with polychromed liturgical inscriptions (*Sanctus, sanctus, sanctus* or *Amen*) —in the front part of the last step—, theological inscriptions (*Panem de coelo eucharistia est*) or devotional inscriptions (*the Holy Sacrament will always be eulogised* written in Catalan). Among the carved symbols three hearts stand out: of Jesus, Mary and Joseph, a reminder, for the artist, of the temple of the Sagrada Família that was being built in Barcelona. The steps are upholstered with green felt.

The lecterns
Oak wood and wrought iron
202 x 112 x 110 cm

For the choral chant, Gaudí built two wrought iron and wood lecterns. Once again we should emphasise the mastery of the wrought iron worker, who stamped beautiful forms onto the hard iron as if it were lead he was working with. The largest, with space for placing four choir books, one on each of its four sides, is quite spectacular. The smaller one only holds two books. The structure of both is in iron: the base and the higher part for supporting the choir books are in oak.

He also cast a faldstool for the master of the chapel, all in iron. It is simpler and lower than the previous two. The high part imitates a grille and the base reminds one of the larger choral lectern.

The pavilion
Wood, bronze and fabric
252 x 124 cm

'La Seu' of Mallorca obtained the title of basilica, applied for by Bishop Campins after the grand restoration of 1904 and awarded by Pope Saint Pius X. On the 1st of October 1905 this distinction was celebrated, also emphasised by the new dedication to the altar. In 1906 the two traditional insignias of the basilica arrived at the episcopal palace: the pavilion (papal umbrella) and the tintinabulum (basilica bell), both designed by Gaudí: not at all conventional, of an original design and creative exuberance. The two basilica insignias are elements of the liturgical processions, presided over by the clergy of the basilica.

The pavilion is conically shaped, like an umbrella or a tent, with alternating strips of red and yellow (gold). Some scholars believe that these were the colours of the medieval papal standard, since the title of basilica is a privilege awarded to a Christian church distinguished by the Roman See. A wooden shaft supports the pavilion, elegantly twisted in the form of an "S", which bears a sphere crowned by a cross on the upper part. The silver-plated crown that rested on it was recovered in 2004 thanks to the Fundació Caixa de Catalunya.

The tintinabulum
Bronze and wood
245 x 18 cm

The tintinabulum is the bell that announces the arrival of the procession of clergymen of the basilica. The bell, designed by Gaudí, is truly original. It does not make a clapper sound in the middle, like conventional bells. A hammer hits it on one of the bronze, almost cylindrical, sides culminated by a radiant sun of the same metal (some suspect that it is polychromed). It is mounted on a wooden stick for carrying on the procession.

Interventions in the episcopal palace

During his time in Mallorca, Gaudí stayed in the Episcopal Palace, which is situated behind the head of 'La Seu'. Gaudí also carried out some work in this building.

The south façade of the Episcopal Palace shows Gaudí's work on a small tower and in several incisions in sandstone carried out on the small windows and window boxes, similar to those he sculpted on the small windows of the sacristies of the chapels in 'La Seu'.

Gaudí's most notable work in the palace is without doubt the series of wrought iron pieces he left there. Firstly of note are the grilles with which he adorned and protected three windows on the east-facing wall: a simple one (a simple cross), and another, a little higher up, in the form of a cross framed by a square. In the upper part is the third and largest window, which also has the form of a cross framed by a square and completed by four iron strips with sinuous movements so typical of Gaudí's wrought ironwork.

In the palace courtyard, over the ogival arches and attached to the west wall, a wrought iron and glass lantern hangs, also attributed to Gaudí, which shows all the characteristic traits of the architect's style. The iron bars and chains form an original and very attractive composition.

Watchtower in
the south façade
of the palace

(next page)
Three grilles
in windows on
the east façade

Details of the stained glass window created by Gaudí in honour of Bishop Campins

Plan of the Catedral

1. Interventions outside the cathedral
2. Large candelabrum
3. Corbels of the Gothic altarpiece
4. Chapel of Saint Bernard
5. Pulpits of the presbytery
6. Galleries for the singers
7. Railing at the entrance of the presbytery
8. High altar
9. Musician angels of the altar
10. Baldachin
11. The new illumination
12. Rose window & two stained-glass windows
13. Choir in the royal chapel
14. Episcopal chair
15. Ceramic decoration
16. Gothic images of the medieval altarpiece
17. Chapel of the Trinity and its royal sepulchres
18. Doorway of Saint Jeronimo
19. Episcopal Palace

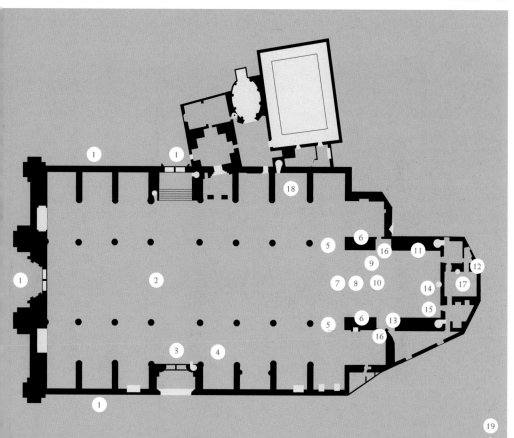

© TRIANGLE POSTALS S.L.

© PHOTOGRAPHY
Jordi Puig, Pere Vivas, Ricard Pla

© TEXT
Pere-Joan Llabrés

© ARCHIVE PHOTOGRAPHS
Cátedra Gaudí, page 40
Arxiu Mas, pages 15, 111

DESIGN
Joan Colomer

LAYOUT
Vador Minobis, Antonio G. Funes

TRANSLATION
Steve Cedar

COLOUR SEPARATIONS
Tecnoart

PRINTED BY
Igol, S.A.
06-2008

DEPÓSITO LEGAL
B-12.345-2005

ISBN
978-84-8478-148-6

Triangle Postals S.L.
Tel.: +34 971 15 04 51, +34 93 218 77 37
Fax: +34 971 15 18 36
www.triangle.cat

We are particularly grateful to the Chapter of
the See of Mallorca for their cooperation in
publishing this book.
© PHOTOGRAPHS: Capítol de la Seu de Mallorca